GOOD GRIEF!

14 Inspiring Stories of Finding the Goodness in Grief

VISIONARY: AYANA HENDERSON

FOREWORD: DR. CHERE M. GOODE

"grief." *American Heritage Dictionary of The English Language, Fifth Edition.* 2022. https://www.ahdictionary.com/word/search.html?q=grief (10 July 2022).

ISBN 13: 978-1-7374212-2-1

ISBN 10: 9781737421

Because of the dynamic nature of the internet, any web addresses or links contained in this book may have changed since publication and may no longer be valid. The views expressed in this work are solely those of the authors and do not necessarily reflect the views of the publisher, and the publisher disclaims any responsibility for them.

Printed in the United States of America

Dedication

This book is dedicated to all those who have experienced loss in any kind of way.
May you find peace that surpasses all understanding and may you find goodness despite your grief.

To my mother who was an avid reader,
may you know that I have turned your loss into a book that will bless generations to come.

To my father, who lived a full life.
One thing you have always shown me was to continue to bless others despite your own pain.
May this be a blessing to others in your honor.

Say not in grief that they are gone, but give thanks that they were yours.

~Hebrew Proverb

Table of Contents

Dedication iii

Foreword 1
By Dr. Chere M. Goode

Introduction 7
By Ayana M. Henderson

The Gift of Good-Bye, Gratitude & Growth 13
By Christal Clair

My Pride...God's Plan 23
By Cyntoria Grant

The Eye of Grace 33
By Jansen Hudson

The Dentist Dealt with My Tooth and the Truth 41
By Charles Irving

If There Is a Will, There Is a Way 49
By Lauren Jarrett

The Church, The Hurt, The Grief, The Grace 59
By Marteka Landrum

Out of the Mouth of Babes 67
Our Young Authors

The Champion Within 69
By Levi Neal

Why Do We Have to Move? 73
By Anaya Neal

People May Not Care, But Don't Let It Stop You 77
By Sekai Neal

Great Times with Grandad 81
By Javon Matthew-Sanders

SuperHuman Strength 85
By Donnie Reed

Me, Motherhood and Grief 95
By Te'Airra Sharma

Prayer of Encouragement 105

Resources 111

Foreword

By Dr. Chere M. Goode

Grief's journey can be one of great sadness, depression, confusion, anxiety, hopelessness, and anger. It is normal to experience one or all those emotions at some point in your healing journey.

Don't beat yourself up. Embrace those feelings and give yourself permission to feel whatever you feel at any given time during your journey. Take as long as you need to heal, however, the worst thing you can do is stay stuck in those negative feelings too long. You may ask, why?

Well, those feelings can fester and become your new norm, which would be detrimental to your mental and physical well-being. You can choose to shift those feelings into something positive. Turning your pain into purpose and finding goodness in the midst of grief.

This book will aid you in finding that goodness. The authors in this book have given real-life examples of finding goodness even while at the lowest points in their lives, during grief.

When I lost my twenty-year-old son Jordan Alexander Cofield in a tragic motorcycle accident on August 22, 2020, followed by the death of his father just 6 months later, life drastically changed forever. The hardest thing after my losses was to just get up and continue with my life. I literally did not want to go on. I felt all the emotions mentioned above at some point or another. Some days I felt all those emotions in one day. The flooding of emotions had me questioning my sanity. It was like being on a rollercoaster ride for many days with the ups and downs of my emotions. I had to make the choice of either getting swallowed up by my grief or making an impact on the world by creating good things out of my tragedies. I chose the latter. I went into immediate action to keep my son's memory alive. I built up a determination to never allow all the positive things my Jordan had done in his short time on this earth to go to waste. I went into action amid my grief and healing.

My mission was to make sure my son's name, legacy, and memory were never forgotten. I turned my sadness and grief to goddess by adopting a roadway in my son's honor, starting a scholarship fund in his honor, and starting a 501c3 non-profit organization. Those initiatives in my late son's honor not only kept me busy but they fueled me to keep living. It feels good to know Jordan will never be forgotten and his legacy will now enrich the lives of others.

I encourage every reader of this book to dig deep within and find those things that bring you happiness, joy, and that good feeling then nurture those things as you heal.

Dr. Chere M. Goode is the Founder/CEO of Total Harmony Enterprises and Make Me Over Wellness. Goode is a mother, caregiver, and the Creator of the Annual RECHARGE Health, Wellness, and Fitness Expo. Goode has been a Licensed Practical Nurse for over 30 years and is Nationally Certified in Hospice and Palliative Care, an area she currently specializes in. Goode is a 5-time #1 Best Selling International Author, Speaker, and Wellness Coach, as well as an American Heart & Stroke Association Ambassador/Spokesperson. Known as the RECHARGE Strategist, Goode teaches professional women strategies for self-care to recharge their Mental, Physical, and Emotional batteries for success in life and business through her 8 Recharge Pillars of Self Care. Goodes's teachings also emphasize the importance of self-care to enrich one's life.

She teaches her clients that if you look good, you feel good so pamper yourself as often as possible. Goode is certified in the relaxation techniques of mindfulness and reflexology. Goode is also the founder of the Ladies Recharge Movement where she hosts quarterly events for women to step away from daily duties to perform self-care and have fun with other like-minded professional women. Goode has been featured on ABC, Dr. Oz, Wendy Williams, Baltimore's TV 25, Good Day Baltimore on Fox 45, Society Moms TV, Radio One, WOLB Radio, Impact The World Radio, I Heart Radio, The Baltimore Times, Baltimore Flava Radio, Impact Nation Magazine and a host of other Magazines and Media Outlets. She has received numerous awards and Government citations for tenacity in business. Most recently she was awarded as a 2020 Woman Thriving in Business and one of Baltimore's Women of Passion, Poise, & Purpose by the Baltimore Times. Goode's expertise in the areas of RECHARGE strategies, self-care, weight management, stress management, mental wellness, and heart disease prevention has touched the lives of many all over the world.

Grief never ends… But it changes. It's a passage, not a place to stay. Grief is not a sign of weakness, not a lack of faith… It is the process of love.

Introduction

By Ayana M. Henderson

When I first considered writing this book I knew that God had a plan beyond what it was going to do for me and my own grief. It was His desire to share how there is goodness in grief despite what we feel or believe. I was about 4 months into grieving the loss of my mom, which was compounded by the death of my father just 16 months before. I hadn't realized the magnitude of loss I was going to feel with both of them gone. I felt like an orphan, even though I was 40 years old at the time.

I was very close to both and as I was going through the journey of loss regarding my mom, and not having her physical presence here with me, God began to show me goodness despite the grief. He began to reveal to me some of the reasons why he allowed it to happen, reasons that were beyond my control but also necessary for me to know. Answers that allowed me to walk in who God called me to be. There are still many unanswered questions, questions I believe He knew I was better off not knowing the answer to.

I learned to accept that. God and God and God will be God, it is what I reconciled.

Good Grief, is a collective of stories of how other grievers championed through their grief. How they were able to overcome and persevere despite feeling such a great loss. There are so many different types of loss. It's not an actual person, place or thing, it's something that you experience as a result of any type of loss that has affected you emotionally, mentally, spiritually, or physically.

As you start to turn the pages of this book I want you to pay close attention to a couple things:

1. Grief doesn't always have to be a loss by death, it can come from any type of loss. I remember when I was going through one of the worst seasons of my life. There I was, looking into the mirror and not recognizing the reflection looking back at me. Her face was dull, the zest and spunk she was known for was gone. She was emotionally and mentally exhausted, and she just looked neglected. I was living up to all these titles, roles, expectations, and standards that others had put on me and I wasn't willing to live up to any of my own. I never lived up to anything I wanted. I had never lived up to anything that I desired. I never

lived up to my own expectations and standards. All of the things I desired, dreamed of, and wanted to accomplish fell by the wayside. And when I came to accept this as truth, I had to grieve the version of myself that I never became and the one that did based on other people's expectations. I had to let go of the things that people had placed on me. I had to let go of the narrative that people spoke over my life. I had to let go of the things that I just didn't achieve because my life went in a different direction. I had also had to grieve the parts of me that never fully healed, the parts of me that were abused and were traumatized. I had to grieve the parts of me that were tucked away for so many years that I didn't even know that they were still affecting me. I had to drive it because I needed to make room to accept who I was and who I was about to become.

2. My hope is that you'll see that grief can be as long as it needs to be but it can also be as short as it needs to be as well. Give yourself permission to recognize that your grief will look different. It will look different in time; it will look different in emotion; it will look different in feeling; it won't even look different in outward expression. A young man I know, who

recently lost his father, had asked his mother if it was weird that he is not crying because his dad died and his mom replied to him, “no, that’s not weird at all. How you process is how you process. Friend, can I sign your grief permission slip? How you process is exactly how you process and that is okay. There’s no time frame, no right way, no wrong way for any type of loss that you’re going through. I remember when I was fired from a job and I was caught off guard, but also not surprised. Sometimes, you just have an inkling in your system that something is about to happen, we just don’t always know the what and the how. When I lost my job I had a really hard time reconciling how this person could let me go in the way that they did. I worked in Human Resources and had mastered the art of firing people. This wasn’t it. I was handled. I was dismissed. I felt disrespected. Considering the working relationship or what I perceived to be our relationship, I couldn’t reconcile what was happening. I understood and accepted intellectually that I no longer had a job but I couldn’t accept and understand where the loss of relationship happened. I had so much respect for this person. It wasn’t until I went to a conference recently and I realized that part of the reason why it was hard for me to move forward was because I hadn't grieved the loss of that relationship. I may never be able to pinpoint when it's the relationship for them changed, but at some point it changed for them and so they made a decision and unfortunately it cost me my job. Once I was able to forgive it and grieve it, I was able to make room for new professional relationships, mentors, and coaches that were gonna come along and push me into my next.

3. Lastly, my hope is that as you're reading this book you can see that you are not alone; that someone else out there has experienced a particular type of loss, your particular type of grief, or your particular type of suffering. It's one thing to be able to express sympathy when someone experiences a loss, but it's an entirely different thing when someone *knows* your type of loss. Inside the pages of this book, there are chapters of people who have shared their specific type of loss and you may find yourself in one of their stores or in one of their types of loss. Each author has shared tangible ways to find the goodness they found despite their grief.

May the pages before you expose your grief. May the pages before you offer grace, may the pages before you offer good company that even in your loss God is still with you. God will always be with us and he will never leave and even though we may not understand the why behind our loss. We still know that He'll use it for our good because he has a perfect plan for our lives and sometimes that includes loss, grief and suffering.

The Gift of Good-Bye, Gratitude & Growth

By Christal Clair

"I've learned that people will forget what you said, people will forget what you did, but people will never forget how you made them feel."

— Dr. Maya Angelou

Grief was uninvited but arrived unannounced to my home at an unsolicited time. At almost three years of age, the dynamics of my family was altered abruptly when my father died suddenly. Because I experienced death so early in life, I understood it to be inevitable and dealt with it differently. As a seasoned woman who experienced the death of my man, the death of my mother, the death of my money, the death of my marriage, and the deaths of men who were my brothers – I feel quite qualified to speak on loss and the grieving process. My losses were unexpected which changed the trajectory of my life in unprecedented manners. *Understanding the Gift of Good-Bye, Gratitude and Growth* were how I learned to cope better and ultimately heal healthier, while witnessing the good in the grief. Hopefully, it will offer a different perspective to you too.

The feelings of grief rarely go away, but in time, the suffering subsides a bit. Death and divorce both represent loss whose outcome is ultimately grief. The great news is that it's perfectly possible that grief can be transformed into good grief, in time. There are multiple genres of grief. Grief is painful. Grief is real. Grief is an individualized experience that no one can attach to a timeline or blueprint because it is different in each instance.

GIFT OF GOOD-BYE

Saying good-bye to a loved one or a relationship can be devastating, distressing, and detrimental to your health. What has crippled you once you exited a relationship? At the same time, there are times when saying good-bye is not a sad or bad thing. Have you ever thought about the good in your good-bye? Take a moment and reflect on your past relationships.

Examples:

Relationship	The Good in Your Good-Bye
Relationship A	Became debt-free and restoration of credit and self-sufficiency
Relationship B	Ability to soar into new experiences and higher heights

I was gifted with an absolutely amazing and generously gratifying relationship that I did not expect. We met at 9:33 p.m. on February 15th on the rail in the skating rink. Our mutual love for skating was what bonded us initially. Our mutual love and excitement about each other is what kept us. We traveled the world and created a life that was a template for others in love. We worshiped together and grew spiritually. There wasn't a time that we argued or weren't intertwined. Life was great! We moved from my place of peace to our love nest. I had never felt so covered and complete as I did with him. A strong man who would cook and clean and remind me that my only job was to "*sit over there and be pretty*." He showered me with compliments and loved me unconditionally. He supported my business endeavors and championed my dreams. After sharing 7 wonderful years together (you do know that the number 7 represents completion and perfection), we began planning to transition into a different and separate relationship and household. This was the most uncertain departure from a relationship that I ever experienced because we did so, while still being in love. It was an endearing agreement that we strategically shifted into, both hesitant while being certain it was time. To this day, we remain two individuals who lovingly communicate, assist one another, travel together, and most importantly laugh often while reminiscing about our everlasting escapades. Although our union concluded, the time together was full of lessons and was a blessing to us both – this was the ultimate gift of good-bye.

We are taught that it takes 21 days to create a habit. For 21 consecutive days, I challenge you to focus on the favorite times; lessons learned; conversations had; and, time shared with those you have grieved over – as a result of death or divorce. Consequently, these memories are ultimately 'gifts.' In a notebook, write the name of your loved one or the experience you have grieved, number your pages daily, and focus on and document one good thought each day, based on the aforementioned. My request is that you revisit what you have journaled on the 27th day and then write a "good-bye" note, indicating the 'gifts' of your relationship – those good things that resulted in you knowing the individual. I believe your focus will shift and that your grief will feel differently.

The gift of good-bye can be an empowering and extraordinary experience.

Examples:

Ma – Day 1	Our weekly road trips to New York and as a result, I still take and love road trips.
Ma – Day 2	Introducing me to and keeping me in church gave me a strong spiritual base
Ma – Day 3	Teaching me "*never to try to fit in since it was obvious I was meant to stand out.*"

GRATITUDE

I am genuinely grateful for the multitude of memories made with each of my loved ones and when I remember them, it helps me to realize just how fortunate I have been to have had them strategically placed in my life. I was assigned the best parents for me and my Mother's strength and resiliency in raising my siblings and I, as a widowed woman taught me how to sincerely show up in life. She unknowingly taught me how to handle grief, graciously.

I wanted my marriage to work and thought it would last forever. I met my husband less than a year after abruptly losing the love of my life. He was what I didn't even know I needed and was unexpected and a 'gift' I learned to be grateful for. He filled voids in my life and we became the best of friends. I sometimes wished we had never married but maintained the friendship instead. I learned early on that "*the one you divorce is never the same person you married.*" I choose to think about the lessons learned and hold on to the great memories we did have together, understanding that our time together had simply expired. I encourage you to remember the good found in those you lost, through death or divorce. In my case, my husband was not a bad person, he simply did not know how to be married to me. The great experiences and time shared absolutely outweighed the bad and I made a conscious decision to remember the good. "Medicine and milk aren't the only things that expire; unfortunately, marriages do too at times." They say, God doesn't close one door without opening another and He didn't disappoint; I'm grateful that life got even better than before.

As the saying goes: "*People come into your life for a*

reason, a season, or a lifetime" and it helped me heal as I reminded myself of that teaching. Try identifying which of the three categories your grief falls in. Identification is one of the first steps to healing.

Examples:

Name or Experience	A Reason	A Season	A Lifetime
My Parents			√
Untimely Unemployment	√		
My Marriage		√	

GROWTH

Resiliency is the result of grief -- we grow stronger. I can honestly say that I learned from each of my loved ones before they passed away and I'd venture to say you did too. I learned how to love fully and unconditionally. Intentionally emulate what you admire and miss the most about what you grieve or who has gone.

Examples:

Name or Experience	What I Admire or Miss	In Memory, I Will . . .
Aunt Jackie	Entrepreneurial Spirit	Grow my business
Wilson	Joy and Laughter	Not be so serious

In conclusion, grieve the loved ones lost and the relationships that died. Grieve the good experiences and grow from your grief. Remember, you're positioned to proceed and always focus on the good in the grief. When you have an opportunity for 'new beginnings' take advantage of them and 'turn your pain into power.' Don't be afraid of change – change is inevitable. This is the chance to identify what really makes you happy; what your non-negotiables are; and, most importantly, to grow by working on yourself. Everything you want in a mate, you should already possess within yourself. If you want someone physically fit, then you should be in shape. If it's important that your mate has good credit and a healthy savings account, then you should have an admirable credit score and be financially fit. If your desire is to be covered spiritually, then you should know more than a few bible verses and be able to pray for someone else. Be the change you want in someone else. Most importantly, never look to a mate to complete or make you happy; others should enhance what you have attained and who you have already grown to be.

"Mindset is mentally major!" Be positive and strive to be better, never bitter. There is life after loss as long as you are open to the possibilities of viewing grief differently. Good grief really does result in growth -- you will be sagacious, spirited, and stronger.

Christal Clair, founder of newly entitled Christal Clear Experiences (CCE) is affectionately known as "The Connector." Christal specializes in showing divorced women how to "pause, pivot, and proceed" into their next chapters. She provides opportunities for women to support women during empowerment and entrepreneurial experiences. For decades, Christal exceeded expectations while creating and managing memorable conferences, meetings, seminars, employee programs and events for thousands of elected officials, financial services leaders, and, 10,000+ transportation professionals, nationally and globally. She is the creator of "Gathering of the Gatekeepers" and "Gathering of the Girls" events. Christal is a #1 Best-Selling Author, Event Producer, and Speaker. To learn more, please follow on Facebook & Instagram at: ChristalClearExperiences or Email: ChristalClearExperiences@gmail.com

My Pride...God's Plan

By Cyntoria Grant

All of you, clothe yourselves with humility toward one another, because, "God opposes the proud but shows favor to the humble." Humble yourselves, therefore, under God's mighty hand, that he may lift you up in due time.

- I Peter 5b-6

How could they do this to me after 15 years of service? I thought. *I helped design and build the office and the work.*

In fall 2008, Mrs. Woods was newly appointed to oversee our office. She came in like a windstorm creating chaos - something we didn't need after a challenging year with her predecessor. She was the new captain of the ship and knew how to rock the boat!

On her department learning tour, in trying to understand our work, she would constantly ask, "What is the work?". She wanted to know not only what we did, but why. We had walked on eggshells for the entire year prior, so our responses were, at best, uncertain. Regardless, I was excited to work for this woman who I partnered with and learned from when my career began.

There was more I could learn under her leadership.

At the start of 2009, Mrs. Woods took the team through a restructuring process. We read Dr. Spencer Johnson's *Who Moved My Cheese*. We questioned her practices, but of course, she had a reason for everything she did. She was on a mission to strengthen the team and the work. She needed to be certain that we wanted to and would adapt to the shifts in the work.

In March, she shared her plan and organization chart and scheduled individual meetings to review the implications. My heart sank as I read and reread the plan. It didn't include me. I found a couple of positions that she may have thought were for me, but I didn't. After all, I worked hard to earn the Director title only for it to be written out. Wasn't I good enough to lead a team? Didn't she see my value? I spent years building this office and my team, and knew how the place ran. We were doing good work. We just needed a little tweaking.

When we met, Mrs. Woods excitedly asked, "Cyntoria, where do you see yourself in the plan?" I said, "I don't, but I have a couple of ideas of where you might." I can still see the look of surprise on her face. She responded, "You don't see yourself right here?" pointing at the organizational chart and role description. I could see the position on the chart, but it didn't have the same title. It wasn't a Director level position. In fact, it was a "demotion". I was silent.

She explained. "I thought you would enjoy this new role. It's exciting and will give you the opportunity to create and envision a new program". I said, "If that is where you see me, that's what I will do". I left with a knot in my throat.

I went home deflated. It didn't matter that I was keeping my salary. I was no longer a director. I was losing my team, my status, and my dignity in one fell swoop. I had become a subordinate within the team I was leading. *How could God allow this to happen to me?*

I went to work daily, depressed. It became harder to face each day as people expressed how sorry they felt. I would close the door to my office and cry. At least I still had my office, but even that was going to be short lived. After a month of trying to adjust, I received a call from Mrs. Woods. Jackie, a person that I used to supervise, would now be my supervisor. "You will have to give up your office and keys." The words hit like a gut-punch taking my breath away. I went home and cried some more.

I had two weeks to move into the cubicle just outside the office. Partners who came, looked at me, then the office and back at me. I smiled and said "all is well". It was my greatest professional disappointment to date at the time. My pastor, the late Bishop Nellie Yarborough, affirmed that I would be ok. My mother also tried to encourage me. I hated going to the place I once loved and sacrificed for.

Late one June afternoon Mrs. Woods sent a meeting request for 8 am the next day in her office. She worked downtown at headquarters, an hour from home. Why couldn't she meet me at my office, 5 minutes from my home? I showed up at the meeting. "Good morning, Cyntoria, close the door and have a seat", she said. She started with the niceties and then said "I don't think you're going to make it. I don't think you are adjusting to your new role." For three minutes it was as if Niagara Falls rushed through my eyes. She waited quietly while I gathered myself. "Give me time," I whispered. "This is hard for me. I need time. I will be ok." When the meeting ended I thought, *She brought me all the way downtown for five minutes. We could have talked by phone.*

I began to pray, "Lord, be my help."

Shortly after, I learned of a one-year graduate-level management program at Suffolk University. Classes were 8 hours on

Thursdays for a year. I applied, not telling anyone, and went on vacation. I thought, *If I am accepted into the program, I will leave my job.*

In August I attended my church's Holy Convocation. I cried at nearly every service. On the last night of service, I cried until the Lord let me know I would be alright and I had to stay where I was. I returned home to an acceptance letter from Suffolk University. I was excited.

Surely Mrs. Woods would not grant a flexible schedule and I would quit. Despite what God told me, I was looking for a way out. I requested permission to adjust my hours and Mrs. Woods excitedly said, "Yes". This threw me for a loop, I anticipated a firm no. I was secretly mad that she was so accommodating of my request. She even had the nerve to ask, "What else do you need? I really want to work with you." All I could muster was,"oh wow, thank you," and left the conversation with a smile.

I started school in September.

In my new role, I did research, and met with partners and other constituents over several different months to create a program by the following June. I was still praying and was still unhappy. I would call my Pastor for her words of wisdom.

Eventually, she would call me daily asking the same question, "How are you doing today?". My response was "depressed and unhappy." She would say, "It will get better." My friend, Mary whose office was in the building where I worked, was also a godsend. When emotions got the best of me I would go to her office, talk and cry, and gather myself. She didn't judge me. Prayers, daily calls, and a safe space for my breakdowns helped me get through the rough patches. Not to mention, I loved my graduate program.

Remember when I asked God why He would allow this to happen? Well, it would be 9 months before He would answer. In December, the Lord spoke to me and said, "You grew too fast and missed some things along the way. You have to go back before you can go forward." His words changed my whole attitude and perspective. It shifted the way I looked at my new job and the challenges it presented. He had given me what I needed, He had given me a process - one filled with grace. The graduate classes focused on managing and creating nonprofits, learning about vision, mission, finances, and leading teams, and boards. All things I did not know but was previously responsible for. I had been practicing leadership on my team and not doing a great job.

This is how God works. A year before everything took

place, I was at a prayer meeting. After we prayed for the sick, a woman began to pray for me. She spoke these words to me, "The Lord is going to humble your heart. You are going to go through something that will cause you to be more humble." I was taken back. In my opinion, I was already pretty humble and never boasted. Little did I know that within a year her words would come to pass.

Going through the process I realized that I let my title define me. My job had taken priority and perhaps made me haughty. I thought I was losing way more than I was gaining. What's more, I was not as good as I thought. I did not have the skills to take the work further. She was right to "demote" me. Humble Pie doesn't taste good. The Lord had to bring me all the way down to build me up.

My program ended in June. What I looked at as a loss, God used to prepare me to take my leadership and work to a higher level. I used everything I learned to create a nationally recognized program, BPS Parent University, now in its 13th year. I eventually received a promotion that later helped me reclaim my title of director, a title I held until I left the organization.

Potters can take clay they want to reform through a "reclaiming" process. They soak it and work with it to reshape it. God, the ultimate potter, sometimes has to reshape us and when he does, we feel loss and grief. When you are grieving such a loss, remember God has a plan for you.

Surround yourself with people who can remind you, when grief causes you to forget. Grieve for the moment, if you must, and then like King David, encourage yourself. When you have nothing left, God is enough. He will fill your cup. Place scriptures on your desk, wall, or phone - reminders that He has you in the palm of your hands. Here are a few I enjoy:

Psalms 9: 9-10 (TLB): All who are oppressed may come to him. He is a refuge for them in their times of trouble. All those who know your mercy, Lord, will count on you for help. For you have never yet forsaken those who trust in you.

Psalms 32: 7-8 (TLB): You are my hiding place from every storm of life; you even keep me from getting into trouble! You surround me with songs of victory. I will instruct you (says the Lord) and guide you along the best pathway for your life; I will advise you and watch your progress.

Ecclesiastes 7:10(KJV): Say not thou, What is the cause that the former days were better than these? for thou dost not enquire wisely concerning this.

Romans 8:28 (KJV): And we know that all things work together for good to them that love God, to them who are called according to his purpose.

1 Peter 5:7 (TLB): Let him have all your worries and cares, for he is always thinking about you and watching everything that concerns you.

Be encouraged. Don't be afraid to ask God, "why are you allowing this to happen to me?" And wait. He'll answer. He always does.

Cyntoria Grant is the Associate Director of Public-School Partnerships at Harvard University.

She leads the team in cultivating strong education-based relationships in Harvard's host communities of Cambridge and Boston and identifying meaningful opportunities to connect Harvard research, faculty, students, and educational initiatives in support of local public schools.

She was the founding director of the nationally known program, Boston Public Schools' Parent University. A program she co-created to support authentic family partnerships in the district.

Additionally, Cyntoria is the Executive Pastor of Berachah Church, where she works alongside the lead pastor to cultivate interactions among the clergy, board, and laity.

The Eye of Grace

By Jansen Hudson

Job stood up and tore his robe in grief. Then he shaved his head and fell to the ground to worship.

—Job 1:20 NLT

We could say that Job standing up and tearing his robe in grief represents his way of expressing and processing his emotions. He was allowing himself to grieve. When he shaved his head and fell to the ground to worship, he was also finding a way to find the goodness in his grief. He made a shift first with his emotions and then with his perspective. It is my desire that Job's right perspective encourages you to not only grieve but to find the goodness in your grief. I experienced something quite similar to Job and perhaps this will help you find the goodness in your grief.

It's in the eye of a tornado that you experience an unexplainable peace. A miracle if you will.

One where you can feel the storms of life swirling all around you, but for just a brief moment, you feel the calm and peaceful presence of God letting you know that He is with you.

For me, that tornado of emotions came on December 21st, when my mother was at church and fell, hitting her head multiple times. My family and I had no idea what happened but became concerned because we hadn't heard from her for hours. We tried calling her, but her phone died. We searched for her for hours and a friend of mine finally found her at the church, it was after midnight. She was outside on the ground fighting for her life. She had been there in the cold, unable to move for six hours. She was eventually airlifted and during the transition, her heart stopped for 10 to 15 minutes.

They revived her and took her to the closest hospital. We found out she was suffering from hypothermia with a body temperature of 70 degrees, pneumonia, frostbite on her left arm, and the bone connected to her right shoulder was completely broken in half. Worst of all, she was not breathing on her own. Thankfully, there was no trauma to the head, but due to the lack of oxygen to her brain when her heart stopped there was some loss of brain activity. She was put in the ICU as soon as she got to the hospital.

At this point, I finally realized I was in a crisis and my emotions were everywhere. However, as soon as I saw her,

I laid my hands on her and prayed for healing and divine protection. I read scripture over her while letting the Bible touch her body. I anointed her with oil and even began to prophesy the word of God over her. I was praying for a miracle.

The staff probably thought I was crazy or felt sorry for me because they thought I was doing what I needed to do to cope with the situation. After six days the doctor told us my mother's blood was shunting. Her feet had turned purple and all the blood was going to her organs. The doctors and nurses told us this was the end. One nurse said, "I've seen miracles before, and this would honestly take a miracle for her to breathe on her own and be conscious." All this was on a Monday and on that day my dad told us he felt in his heart to wait until Thursday to take her off life support.

Everyone around me had given up and lost hope besides myself and my husband. And I can see why they lost hope. Part of me was wanting to lose hope too but the other part of me kept praying. During this time of prayer, God gave me a deeper understanding of what it means to truly pray for his will rather than the comfort of my own pain. No longer was I praying for my mom to live so I wouldn't have to feel pain, but praying for God's will to heal her so her story could give him glory. If she were healed, people would know that only He alone could have healed her and in return, people could turn to God and souls could be saved. The eye of the storm came when I found goodness by learning to worship God in the midst of this crisis.

When Wednesday came around, I drove to the hospital crying uncontrollably thinking about it was going to be the last day I get to talk to my mom and wondering what my last words would be. I had come to the realization that this was the end.

But, let me tell you about my Jesus! I was the first person in my mother's room that day and as soon as I walked in the doctor immediately came in and said to me, "ma'am you cannot take her off life support tomorrow. She is breathing on her own. We are just giving her a little oxygen and all the blood has gone back to her feet." The nurse explained that medically speaking, she couldn't explain any of this. She stated, "this is the miracle you have been praying for." I was in awe. I ran through that hospital praising God. He literally performed a miracle. We were ecstatic. The next day, instead of taking her off life support, I walked into my mother's room and she was sitting straight up, eyes wide open, coherent, with no tubes down her, and breathing on her own. She was talking to us as best as she could. She was moved to her own room and everyone was hopeful. We saw up close and personal the working of God's hand. We felt like we were in peace and calm, we were in His grace, mercy, and favor, even if it was just for a little bit.

The next night, she realized how helpless she was and knew it would not be an easy recovery. She told my dad she wished she would have gone on to live with Jesus. I'm not going to lie, I was so mad that she said that. Although later I realized that life can wear and tear some people down so much that they get tired and she was definitely tired. My mom had been through a lot of hardships in life. The following night, we got a call that she was back in ICU due to her low oxygen level and she was put back on life support. She had prayed for God to take her to her heavenly home. She didn't want to fight. God had done his part, but she didn't want to do hers. Instead of being mad at her, I was just sad for her.

On January 3rd, 2022, we respected my mother's wishes and took her off life support, and in just 80 minutes, she was gone. Watching her struggle to breathe was the hardest thing I've ever had to do. My heart was shattered. How was I going to live in a world where the person who gave me existence no longer existed?

I guess you may be asking where is the goodness in all this? And it was that God was truly glorified by the miracle he performed. My family and I can tell her story and give him the glory. This entire experience is only part of how I found goodness in my grief. The goodness I found didn't stop there.

When I grieved and cried for my mother, I would remember who she was and how special she made me feel. I've learned that the way to deal with the pain is to face it. This is the only way to heal. Some people are afraid to heal because they believe if they hold on to the pain they are holding on to the person they lost and to let go of that pain would be to let go of or forget that person. When I say heal, I don't mean get over it or forget the person, I mean heal so that the pain doesn't consume you leaving you traumatized and unable to move forward in this life you still have to live in.

Give yourself permission to go to the bathroom or to your car to feel, cry, journal, talk to God, or even to the person who passed away. It's healthy to say out loud or to write down what you want to say to the person you are grieving. Whether it's angry words or loving words it will make you feel better afterward. Lastly but most importantly, lean on God during this time of grief and rest in him. I want to encourage you to allow yourself to be vulnerable before God. Go to him with an honest approach. Tell him exactly how you feel even if you are angry with him. Tell him everything. He is longing to show you his goodness during your time of grief. But the question is, will you let him? I have discovered that for me personally the goodness in my grief was when I came to the end of me and found Jesus.

Jansen Hudson is a mental health coach, counselor, and transformational teacher. She helps leaders live a purposeful life by developing healthy belief patterns. She believes that

shifting thoughts and having the right perspective is key to living a purposeful and enjoyable life. Jansen currently resides in Middle Tennessee. She loves spending time with her family, resting in the presence of God, and practicing self care.

You can follow her on Facebook @JansenHudson.

To learn more about her grieving process or healthy belief patterns you can connect with her via email at jansenhudson33@gmail.com or direct message her on facebook @JansenHudson.

The Dentist Dealt with My Tooth and the Truth

By Charles Irving

The American Heritage Dictionary describes grief as deep mental anguish, as that arising from bereavement. But, while studying grief and learning to grieve I've come to realize; grief is also a healing and transformative process.

I remember when the Holy Spirit showed me I needed to grieve an experience that planted something inside me, I didn't even know was there. I was at the dentist getting two cracked teeth removed. One tooth was in the back of my mouth on the right, and the other tooth was directly across from it on the left. I hated going to the dentist, so for a while, I didn't deal with it. Eventually, more pieces cracked and broke off, which forced me to address the situation. After about a year of not dealing with it, I finally went to the dentist to have those cracked teeth removed. The dentist came in the room while I was sitting in the chair, injected Novocain in my gums on the right side of my mouth, left, and came back about 10 minutes later. He put the chisel in my mouth and pried my tooth out with no problem. He injected Novocain on the left side of my mouth, left the room, and came back about 10-15 minutes later. He put the chisel in my mouth and began prying out my tooth. I jumped and screamed, "Ughhh!" He said, "You can feel that?" Slurring my words, I said, "Yeah, I can feel that!" He said, "Oh, let's use some more Novocain."

He put more Novocain in my gums, left for several minutes, came back, and tried it again. I screamed, "Ughhh!" He said, "You can feel that?" I said, "Yes, I can feel that!" He injected more Novocain. He put 6 vials of Novocain in my mouth, which is the legal limit. This time, he left for about 30 minutes. When he came back and went to pry the tooth out of my mouth, I could still feel the pain. Amazed, he said "You can feel that?" Frustrated, I said, "Yes I can feel that!" He said, "Man, I don't know what to tell you! Maybe we should do this another day." I said, "No, we have to deal with this." He said, "Are you sure?" I said, "You have to get this out of my mouth. I can't continue on like this. I have to deal with it."

He went in and began to pry my tooth out, and I could feel everything. I could hear the ripping of the tooth from my gums. I could feel the tearing in the back of my neck. It was excruciating. The procedure only lasted about 45 seconds, but it felt like 45 minutes. When it came out, I felt immediate relief. Although I was shaking because of the adrenaline, I didn't feel the pain anymore. He said, "Man, I'm going to let you sit here for a minute because that was traumatic. I've never seen anything like that. The dentist and his assistant left. As I sat there trying to calm myself down physically, I began feeling this deep sorrow well up within me. I thought, *What is that*? Naturally, I mentally process a lot, so going into a processing mode is normal for me regardless of what I am dealing with at the moment. Instead of allowing myself to feel what I was feeling, I began asking myself questions, trying to figure out what was going on. I was afraid I was about to have what I thought might be a mental breakdown. I had never had one before, but I knew something was wrong. The more I started to process, the more my emotions began to shift. Right then, I heard the Spirit of the Lord say, "Stop, I need you to feel this!"

I knew what He was saying. If you process through this, you're not going to feel it. You *need* to feel this. However, I was terrified of what might happen if I allowed myself to do that. I didn't want to go somewhere emotionally I had never been, and I wasn't sure how I could come out of that place. Whatever was there, I didn't want to know what it was. I didn't want to acknowledge or face it. I just wanted to fix it without having to feel it, but I knew God was with me, and that gave me the peace to let go of the idea of needing to be in control. I sat back, allowed what felt like an avalanche of sadness to wash over me, and wept from the depth of my soul. That moment afforded me the opportunity to get something out that had been there for decades. I was hurt, but I had suppressed it subconsciously for years. I got to the point where I knew my emotional release was near the end. I prayed, "God what is this?" The Spirit said, "I couldn't allow you to go on like this any longer. You've tried to use so many things to numb the pain you endured as a child. You used relationships to numb the pain. You've used sex to numb the pain. You've used anger to numb the pain. You've used so many things to numb the pain. I couldn't allow you to go on any longer trying to numb the pain. It would have killed you."

Shortly after He spoke, I began getting a revelation that connected my childhood to why I ended up in the dentist's chair. I became aware of the fact that I couldn't remember a routine doctor's visit. I couldn't remember a routine dental appointment from when I was a kid. Why is this important? It's important because when you become an adult, you do what your parents taught you when you were a kid. That's how you learn to take care of yourself. At that moment, I realized everything I had just experienced in that dental chair could have been avoided.

However, because I had never learned to go to the dentist routinely, and only went when absolutely necessary, I created a problem with my oral health. Subsequently, I was sitting in the dentist's chair as an adult with 2 teeth removed that I never would get back. I sat there devastated, as I said to myself in awe, "I was neglected." At that moment, I realized I was grieving years of pain and loss as a result of childhood neglect. I had never allowed that truth to come from my mouth until that moment. God allowed me to experience the ineffectiveness of numbing my gums, as a metaphor, to help me understand what I was doing to myself by numbing to suppress the pain. I had been numbing the pain to cope with how I felt for decades and didn't know it.

Acknowledging the truth was painful, but it also was validating.

By denying the significance of what happened and suppressing it, I was denying it mattered to me. By denying it mattered, I unconsciously was telling myself I didn't matter. I needed to grieve the pain of neglect to validate the truth of my own importance. Grieving the matter unconsciously sent the message to me that I mattered. There was a great sense of release and relief, in grieving the grief, that I had never experienced before. I left the dentist feeling lighter, happier, at peace, and with an air of excitement. Sure, I lost something I couldn't get back, but by the grace of God, I was allowed to experience the goodness of grief because I gained something I wouldn't have otherwise: Freedom.

Grieving the grief allowed me the transformative opportunity to acknowledge the wound, feel the pain, and begin the process of healing so that I could be whole again.

Charles Irving is a husband, father, and founder of COACH'DbyCharlesIrving.

COACH'DbyCharlesIrving is a program dedicated to teaching men and women how to emotionally heal and become whole by helping them build a better relationship with themselves, so they can experience the freedom and peace they deserve. Charles Irving was born and raised in Boston Massachusetts, but now, he lives in Atlanta, Georgia.

Charles would love to hear from you!

Feel free to follow him on IG @coachdbycharlesirving and share your journey of how you are using this book to help you build a better relationship with yourself.

The only cure to grief is to grieve.

~ Earl Grollman

If There Is a Will, There Is a Way

By Lauren Jarrett

The LORD watches between me and thee when we are absent from one another.

(Genesis 31:49)

When I lost my mom, I had no idea that I would eventually lose my stepfather, Ron. It wasn't through death, but the relationship certainly died with the loss of my mom. It affected me so badly, that I don't even regard him as "stepfather" anymore. He has been demoted to "my mother's widower."

My mom–who I will affectionately refer to as "Mommy"-- and I were always close. She worked full time as a schoolteacher making sure I was well taken care of. Mommy always let me know how much she loved me and made it clear that I could share anything with her, without judgment. "You can do anything in the world you want to do," she told me, and I always believed her. She was the most genuine human I've ever known. As I grew older, I could call her for advice on just about anything–career, relationships, cooking… Outside of God, I trusted that she would help guide me in life to the best of her ability.

My first two years of life, it was just me and Mommy. Then she met Ron and they eventually got married six years later. I remember our household being one of love and laughter, with periodic road trips for vacation or to visit family. Although Ron and I may have disagreed here and there over the years, we got along for the most part.

When I was in 5th grade, our lives took a turn when Mommy experienced a nearly fatal pulmonary embolism. With only a third of her lung capacity remaining, she was permanently placed on oxygen along with a laundry list of medications. Any trip outside of the house warranted the need for a portable oxygen tank to keep her always connected. Periodic hospital stays became a regular part of our lives.

Reluctantly, Mommy had to take disability retirement from her love and passion of teaching because her condition prevented her from being able to withstand the demands of moving around the school and speaking in front of her classes all day. Our new normal meant having to wake myself up and get myself ready for school. Before I learned to drive, she would drive me to the grocery store and send me inside with a list and money. Ron and I mostly split household duties between each other.

When I went off to college (out of state), Ron became mommy's primary caregiver. There were tasks Mommy was still self-sufficient at such as, driving herself to a doctor or hair appointments–if there wasn't a long walk. She could still bathe and dress herself, and cook or bake, while mostly sitting. All in all, they both supported me in my early adulthood self-discovery phase and wanted me to enjoy life and be happy. I am grateful to them for that.

In early 2008, 14 years after that pulmonary embolism, Mommy was diagnosed with Pulmonary Hypertension–high blood pressure in the blood vessels that supply the lungs. It's a serious condition that affects arteries in the lungs and the right side of the heart. They gave her from 6 months to 2 years to live. I think she knew and felt that she would be on the lower end of that spectrum. Mommy seemed to be in the hospital a little more than usual that year–some of the times, she wouldn't even tell me for fear of worrying me.

By the summertime, I was on the phone with her even more than our usual daily chats and I could tell that her health was deteriorating. I was living in Washington, DC, and she was in Indiana. I promised that I would get home to see her in October for my birthday, but she needed me to come sooner. It hit me hard that my mother was dying and there was nothing I could do about it, even though I tried. I fasted for a stretch of time; I prayed long and hard. My uncle, who also lived in DC, told me that we were going to drive up for Labor Day weekend for a visit. We went straight to the hospital upon arrival. I had a moment to sit with her, just us two, and she filled me in on her prognosis. Meanwhile, she emphasized that no matter what happened, that I remain strong and live my life. She told me that whatever belonged to her, I could have, but she especially wanted me to have this particular, quality-made Brumby rocking chair/footrest set in which to rock my children one day. I said, "OK, but promise me one thing. If you decide to go, please come visit me in my dreams." "I will," she said.

We spent the whole final day of our stay with her, took some photos and said our good-byes. Once I left the room I sat in a chair in the hallway and just wept. I knew it was the last time I was going to see my Mommy. Two days later, I called to speak to her but one of my cousins answered the phone saying that she wasn't feeling great and could I call her back. On September 3, 2008, I got the dreaded call from Ron while at work, "Your mama's passed." My world was shattered. I instantly felt alone. Yet, oddly enough, I felt a sense of relief in the midst of the agony. Mommy was no longer suffering and in pain, and I no longer had to constantly worry about her anymore.

However, I felt bad for Ron, losing a spouse of nearly 20 years and being left in an empty house to grieve and figuring out how to "move on." Over the next 7 years, he would remind me that if I wanted anything out of the house I grew up in, it would be there for me whenever I was ready. I didn't have to be in a rush since I didn't yet have a house of my own.

In 2015, I was scrolling on Facebook, when I came across a post of a mutual friend where a woman with whom I went to high school commented. I noticed she had the same last name as Ron. Upon doing further research, I learned that Ron married this woman with whom I went to high school and 26 years his junior. "WTF?!" is all I could think to myself.

Shortly thereafter, I called him to say that it was time to get my belongings, not letting on that I knew about his recent marriage. We agreed to meet a few weeks later to go through the belongings. When I arrived at the house, instead of inviting me in, we stood in the driveway. During the entire visit, I never saw the inside of the house. Ron would bring things out to the garage or yard for me to sort through and pack. Some items I would ask for, he gave me a firm "no." There is jewelry that belonged to my mom and grandparents that would be wonderful to share with my children one day, but he was adamant about not releasing any of it. Here's the kicker, Mommy did not have a will and Indiana law states that if there is not a will in place, then the surviving spouse takes possession and has governance over all personal property left behind. I was screaming in frustration and fury on the inside. Remember the rocking chair Mommy specifically wanted me to have? He didn't give it to me. I left with some photos, some clothes, kitchen items and a few mementos from her early teaching days, but that's about it. That was the day our relationship ended. He and I haven't spoken since.

Allegedly, Ron still has a bunch of items in storage, including the chair and jewelry. I'm at a point in my life now where I have learned to release ties to material things. I find more value in the photos, and vivid memories/dreams that I have of Mommy. Quite frankly, I have been without those "things" all this time, what difference does it make to have them now?

A spiritual medium once told me that Mommy wants me to know that even though she misses me through the physical realm, she is much better able to watch over and protect me in the spiritual. Wow! How strong and sacred is a mother's love that she would find death to be the best way to stay close and protect her child?! That message totally changed how I perceive death and the afterlife. I have found comfort in the belief that Mommy continues to be present in ways far beyond her abilities in the flesh and is constantly protecting me and now her grandbabies as well. That's all I can really ask for. The scripture that is at the beginning of this chapter, is actually one half of a charm that both me and Mommy wore, and I still wear my half today. I was not able to collect her half, but God has kept her with me. As for Ron, I forgive him. Not for him, but for me. He shall reap what he has sown, and I am OK with that.

I share this to highlight the importance of having a will. There was an opportunity for me to have generational possessions that my mother verbally granted me in her death, but not having it in writing put those invaluable possessions in the hands of someone who couldn't understand or appreciate the value they held for me. I'll never know if he held them out of spite, but what I do know is that had a will been in place, I would have all that she truly wanted me to have in her death. My advice to anyone reading this, have a will!

One of the quickest ways to establish something in writing, is to send an email to a loved one letting them know this serves as a will until one can be drafted by an attorney.

You can type one up, have it notarized and mail it to a loved one until you are able to have one legally drafted. No matter how much you think you know and trust someone, please have a will in place and encourage your loved ones to do the same.

Lauren is a Wellesley College alumna who works as a real estate agent/investor and Massage Therapist. She is an entrepreneur at heart and stays busy working on bringing her business ideas to fruition. She is passionate about helping others wherever possible while spreading love in the process, hence her company name RE-build Love LLC. Lauren loves family time, writing, cooking/baking, music, traveling and being outdoors (especially the beach!). She currently lives in Atlanta, Georgia, with her husband Lee and their two boys. You can connect with Lauren via Instagram @isellbighouses & @rebuild_love_rei

Grief is in two parts. The first is loss. The second is the remaking of life.

~ Anne Rophie

The Church, The Hurt, The Grief, The Grace

By Marteka Landrum

"Then tears streamed down Jesus' face."

John 11:35 TPT

I've heard it said that the pressure changes when God is about to take you to another level. I missed the warning to fasten my seatbelt and hold on for a bumpy ride. What ride do you ask? The fifteen-month period where I transitioned from being a youth leader to accepting, training, working as a children's pastor, and being fired. Who gets fired from a church?

On paper I had two part-time jobs:

-job share at a large urban elementary school in 3rd grade

-a missionary position at an inner-city church as a Children's Pastor

The reality was each required a different kind of prep work. In all my leadership training prior to being on staff at this church, it was made clear that the buck stops with you.

First and foremost give your best to the Lord. Perfection is not expected however excellence is. If you're not going to give Him your best, don't do it. As the leader, you are responsible. You don't need to try to do it all. It is up to you to make sure everything gets taken care of.

So, I was taking care of business. My teaching partner and I had divided up the week, had our communication system down, and knew who was teaching what. I worked to stay on top of my tasks during the days I was there so I wouldn't get behind. There were Children's events Sunday through Thursday. I coordinated: drivers for the bus; volunteers for tutoring, Kid's Club, and Nursery; snacks for tutoring and Kid's Club; whole and small group lessons for Kid's Club; summer activities, and seasonal events. I did this while also raising financial support because this was a missionary position. Yes, I was burning the candle at both ends. I made it known at the church that this position required a team of people. One person could not do it all very well. I spent many late nights at the church because it was quiet, there were no interruptions, and because I work best late at night. Things needed to be prepped for the next time kids would be there. In addition to this, I still had all the regular activities at the elementary school.

To make matters worse, my cousin died. He was two years older than me. We grew up spending lots of time together. His death really shook me up so much I took a week off from work.

At both jobs, we were now beginning to transition to summer mode, which included, year-end testing, promotions, discussions about summer camp, and ending programs and school. We were in a staff meeting with a few of the Elders. They began asking me questions about volunteers and parents that I didn't know the answer to. This is when things became uncomfortable. I was trying to process what is really going on, and feeling confused I was not hearing everything clearly. I didn't even know there was a problem, but by their tone and questioning there clearly was one. I told them this was the first I had heard about these concerns. I said I would look into it and that I needed time after investigating to pray for direction. Based on the questions, I felt as though they were building a case against me. The more questions they asked, the more I could tell they had already decided. I asked to wait until after my scheduled vacation to come back with a resolution to their concerns. Finally, they said, "We have made a decision….. please turn in your keys Friday."

I don't remember all that was said. But I do remember

my response was, "Well so be it but I'm not turning in keys on Friday. I have to finish getting registrations for the various camps. I will turn in my keys by the end of the month." Over the next several days, I was in a brain fog. I was in total shock but I still had to teach 3rd grade and be a Children's Pastor. The next two weeks felt like I was going through all the stages of grief at the same time: shock, anger, bargaining, denial, and acceptance. Of all the questions they were asking, not one of them had to do with a child or programming. These were adult issues.

I learned to never meet without taking a witness. As I was finishing out my work, I had a meeting with the Senior Pastor and one of the Elders. It was horrible. During my last month, I was still expected to have my report for the Board meeting and be in attendance. I decided to take not one, but two trusted men with me. I was very professional in my black dress and pearls with my hair pulled back. We went in with a mission. I was **not** going to be run over again. I really did not like being the mature one in all of this. Somebody needed to be and it really was the grace of God. I talked calmly. During this meeting I was asked to write a letter to the church, supporters, and volunteers that I would be leaving my role. I wrote a letter to the church telling them when my last day would be. I wrote letters to supporters and all volunteers explaining I would not be continuing. The Lord told me I had to finish all letters and have them mailed before I leave for vacation. I asked Him why I have to do all this. He said simply, "It's the right thing to do."

Sometimes I get tired of being the one doing the right thing. Why couldn't I just walk away? Why did I have to be the bigger person? I learned so many lessons from this experience.

A saving grace was that I already had a trip planned. Once the letters were finished and had been dropped off at the post office, I was free. It was great to leave it all behind. While on vacation, I chose to lean into the Lord. I was told, "Part of your healing will come through your tears. Do not hold back. You responded correctly by taking care of the little lambs." When I returned, I leaned into God even more.

There were three things the Lord had me do: rest, reflect, and read. Thankfully I was already in therapy as well. As part of the reflection, I wrote more letters over the next few months. Most of them were the kind you don't mail. The point of these letters was to label my emotions and deal with them.

When I rested in the Lord, I chose to trust Him and each day I asked Him what to do. I didn't know what was going to happen to my finances. I had a mortgage to pay. I was in no shape to get a job. I was devastated emotionally. I had recently come face to face with my own mortality and now this felt like ultimate rejection. Who gets fired from being a Children's Pastor and no children were harmed? The first thirty-one and a half years of my life had been marked by lack and lots of fears. The last eighteen months had been marked by Jesus preparing to heal me of lack and all those fears. I knew in August school would start again. It was too late to get out of the job share even though I needed to be full-time. The Lord began to unravel some wrong thoughts I had. My identity was not in being a teacher. My identity was in being His daughter.

That summer, I learned who I was, how to do self-care and to rest. I continued to go to therapy, journal, pray, and read. I read the Bible as well as other inspirational books. Almighty God is such a good, good Father. He took such good care of me that summer and the rest of the year.

If you have experienced church hurt, you are not alone. The best advice I can give you is to learn how to rest in God by giving your situation or circumstances over to Him. You can get a journal and write to God about how you are feeling or write letters that don't get mailed to express your hurt. And lastly, get in the Word. Read about how much God loves you and who He designed you to be because that is where your true value and identity are. And just to have extra support, get a therapist. Worshiping Jesus plus therapy was a game-changer.

There is a silver lining. At a community event, six years later, the Senior Pastor apologized saying they did it all wrong. I was speechless but very thankful for the apology. God's love, mercy, and favor are always with us.

Marteka Landrum is a coach for challenging teens. She works with schools and parents by meeting teens where they are at to help them understand how their actions are impacting others, get clear on who they are, and give them coping and communication strategies so that they can finally feel understood, have success in school, and have better relationships so everyone can find peace.

Marteka enjoys helping others find their truth, loves to cook, sing and travel. Connect with her at www. positivechanges11.com or on Instagram and Facebook @ positive_changes11.

Out of the Mouth of Babes

Our Young Authors

The next four mini chapters are from young people who experienced loss in their own way.

Here how they were able to find goodness in their own loss.

Ages 10 to 22

We want to go through our grief and not around our grief.

~Griefshare

The Champion Within

By Levi Neal

Ayana: What type of loss did you experience?
Levi: Losing a basketball game

Ayana: What happened that you lost the game?
Levi: We were playing against all these good teams and we were like the worst team. We lost our point guard. We had to make adjustments like moving our power forward to the point guard position and he did that while playing center. We had less players and this one game, it was only me and one other player scoring .We lost that game 45-17.

Ayana: What was one good thing that came out of losing that game?
Levi: It was the fact that I scored 15 points, my highest I ever scored in a basketball game.

Ayana: How did it make you feel even though you lost the game hardly make you feel when you realize how many points you actually scored?
Levi: Proud of myself

Ayana: What is one thing you would tell other young boys who experienced losing a game?

Levi: Keep going for your goals. Don't give up and always try your best.

Levi is the friend you go to when you need help. Always willing to lend a hand to help, you can find Levi in the classroom helping his friends with homework, reading and having fun. Leave loves to learn and is never afraid to ask questions. Levi has a great sense of humor, loves basketball, Fortnite, 2K NBA, and football.

He currently lives with his family in Georgia.

Grief is love's unwillingness to let go.

Why Do We Have to Move?

By Anaya Neal

Ayana: What was one person, place, or thing that you feel like you have lost?

Anaya: Leaving where I grew up. Boston, MA.

Ayana: What do you feel like you lost or what do you feel like you miss the most about Boston?

Anaya: My family, my cousins, my friends

Ayana: What did it feel like when you were leaving Boston?

Anaya: It was upsetting because I really didn't feel like I had a choice. I have to go wherever you go. I didn't want to go to a new school where I would be the new girl.

Ayana: What challenges did you face in Atlanta?

Anaya: The transition from elementary school to middle school was probably the hardest transition, it took a couple of months for me to adjust. The weather was one of them and the fact that they didn't have any snow or enough snow especially around my birthday and missing out on all the family gatherings because we don't really have any family down here.

Ayana: Once you got to Atlanta what shifted in you to be okay with moving from Boston? What made Atlanta okay?
Anaya: Waffle House, I got my own room again after having to share with my mom and brother for a year. I also made a lot of new friends at my new school and was still able to keep in touch with my cousin and some of my friends in Boston.

Ayana: What is one thing you feel like you have gained as a result of moving?
Anaya: I was able to establish boundaries because I now had my own space to just be.

Anaya is a typical middle school girl who loves all things TikTok, Snap Chat, nails and fashion. Anya enjoys listening to music, watching movies and hanging out with her mom. As a winter baby, she loves the snow. Although she wishes she was still in Boston, she currently lives in Georgia with her family.

Do not resent yourself for how slowly you are healing. It takes time and you need to remember that.

People May Not Care, But Don't Let It Stop You

By Sekai Neal

Ayana: What type of loss did you experience?

Sekai: My first basketball game. It was my first game in seventh grade.

Ayana: What was that like for you to experience this type of loss?

Sekai: I thought that I did well in that game, but when it was over, nobody really noticed or cared about my performance.

Ayana: How did you process feeling this way?

Sekai: I cried. It was a temporary relief and release that allowed me to move on.

Ayana: Did you feel like it was your fault?

Sekai: Not really. I felt like there was nothing else I could've done.

Ayana: Who were the people who believed they didn't care?

Sekai: The people there. The spectators. My Coach.

Ayana: What did this experience teach you yourself, the game or spectators?

Sekai: To keep going, keep trying. You are going to take a lot of losses before you get a win., eventually you will get there.

Ayana: What was one good thing that came out of that experience?

Sekai: I learned that not everyone is going to care and that's ok. You just have to do what you have to do. I just have to focus on playing my game.

Ayana: How did this loss develop you as a ballplayer?

Sekai: I no longer focus on the looks, I just execute on all that is given to me and do what I have to do to help the team. I'm a better team player because of this. I also stopped worrying about stats.

Ayana: What is one piece of advice you would give another young man who lost his first game after feeling like he played well yet no one noticed him?

Sekai: People noticing you is not going to matter in the long run. Go to your coach and see how you can become better and practice, practice, practice.

Sekai is an avid gamer and loves basketball. Acquiring knowledge is one of his greatest assets. He enjoys helping others, sharing jokes, and developing his skills on and off the court. He is currently in high school and lives just northeast of Atlanta, GA with his family.

Grief is like the ocean: it comes on waves, ebbing and flowing. Sometimes the water is calm, and sometimes it is overwhelming. All we can do is learn to swim.

~Vicki Harrison

Great Times with Grandad

By Javon Matthew-Sanders

Ayana: What type of grief do you want to talk about?
Javon: Losing my grandfather

Ayana: How did that make you feel?
Javon: It was very tough losing someone that you always talk to. It's definitely the hardest when there's some things that you know you just can't talk to anyone else about. He was the person I would go to for things like that. He was that one person that always had good advice. It's still hard. I'm still working through it.

Ayana: What was the experience like for you going through losing someone important for the first time?
Javon: It was sad. I was angry that he was gone. I was losing that one part or piece in my life. I knew I had grown so close to him, he was like my best friend. The one person you could really talk to whatever time and for whatever you need. He was always there.

Ayana: What have you found has helped you get through

grieving him?

Javon: I would remember the memories and good times and the laughs and the parties, and the cookouts. That we always have a fun time with him, especially all the advice he gave me.Making sure that whatever advice he gave me throughout life I'm still using.

Ayana: For anybody who may have lost a grandparent that they were really close to, what is one piece of advice that you could share with them that would help them deal with the loss?

Javon: To not focus on the should've, could've, would've scenarios or any changes or adjustments you would have made. Think of the good times and memories, the things that they may have taught you, or some lessons that you learned and then put those to good use.

Ayana: What is one good thing that came out of losing granddad?

Javon: That he was at peace and I had learned a lot from him. He was at peace with what he did in his life and his journey.

Javon developed a strong work ethic at the age of 3 from working alongside his grandfather and has been working ever since. A native of Boston, he loves his home teams and will always ride for always. He loves making people laugh, public speaking, and all things cars and sneakers.

Javon currently resides near Atlanta, GA with his family.

Grief does not change you…it reveals you.

~John Green

SuperHuman Strength

By Donnie Reed

"When my father and my mother forsake me, then the Lord will take me up." Psalms 27:10 KJV

Being born in the early 80's in Boston, Massachusetts was tough. Heroine was a leech sucking the life's blood out of the black community and crack ushered in a new wave of affliction. The last thing my mother or father had time for was to love me.

Their sole mission of the day was to feed their ever starving addictions. A seed never grows where it is not watered and I was sown into the plight of my mother, and harvested from her field of tribulation. The love and affection she eagerly attempted to give wasn't enough to negate the neglect I was subjected to. My days were like midnight, dark and lonely and my nights were bright like the sun in the middle of July, there was no shade for sleep.

I was often left alone as a young child. I can still taste the tears I shed by the window waiting and wishing for my mother to return. Tears that I never knew God was collecting for my good. These moments of my life are more vivid than a Martin Scorsese film.

I remember waking up at night to the sounds of horror and scenes of the living dead. My father was long gone by this time. Although, his absence didn't hurt as much as the pain my mother inflicted on my young heart day to day.

However, God has a love thing for me, so he sent a trusted servant on a special assignment to enrich the soil of my life; he was using the tears from my childhood so that one day He'd use them to help me bear fruit to feed generations to follow.

Her name was Angela P. Hester, aka Nanny, who was my great-grandmother. The person whose wisdom, commitment, grace, strength, sacrifice, and her relationship with God molded and shaped me into the man I am today. The moment she rescued me from the grips of chaos and calamity, she brought me straight to God to be cleansed. She began teaching me the principles and values she lived by. Which were strength, resilience, intelligence, honesty, grace, faith and honor.

From the ages of 10-17, I lived with her and learned under her tutelage. Although, outside of her watchful eye, I lived a worldly life and made catastrophic mistakes. Her greatness came with lofty expectations I wasn't ready to live up to. The value system she'd put in place, was nullified by the cross I bore.

I didn't feel the love from the parents who birthed me. I felt alone and unwanted. I was battered, bruised and broken. The tears I cried at night were enough to overflow a levy. Until anger and resentment replaced those tears and numbed my pain. I wasn't good enough for them, so I sought affirmation from the streets. Which ultimately led me to being expelled from high school and fathering my first daughter, Destinea, at 18 and my second daughter, Essence, 8 months later.

Though they were a bright spot in my life, the things I had to do to feed them weren't. In the midst of perpetuating a fraud and being someone I wasn't called to be, Nanny was called home to be with God in 2003. Her assignment was complete and I was so hurt. I had become broken all over again. I couldn't fathom life without her here. So riddled with anger and despair, I immersed myself deeper into the streets.

Early Christmas morning in 2005, a few of my comrades and I almost lost our lives to gun violence. Days later, I was arrested and incarcerated for firearm charges among prior violations. Nanny came to me in a dream my first night in bondage and gave me her first of many messages from heaven.

"Boy, until you go back to God, your life will never be the same again."

When I look back over my life and all I've overcome, I thank God for all that I've been through. My pain activated my super power. I overcame the obstacle of grief by using one of the many core principles taught to me growing up. Which was spirituality. Nanny ran to God in times of trouble, she felt no one could ease her stress the way God could. Romans 8:28 (NIV) it says, "And we know that in ALL things God works for the good of those who love him, who have been called to his purpose."

Once I wrapped my adult mind around this truth, my childhood and losing Nanny were no longer a hindrance. They became fuel.

At 15, I fell in love with Hip Hop, as did a great majority of my generation. So much so, it inspired me to strive to become a MC or rapper. But I discovered, not only did becoming an artist make me cool, it was also a conduit for me to express my pain. Often my peers would mention that my music was dark. I'd reply by saying, "this artform is self expression." In the words of Langston Hughes, "life for me ain't been no crystal stair."

As I grew in my craft, I discovered that words were my actual gift. Whether it was writing music, poetry and now even books, I can use my pain to fuel my creativity. More importantly, I found my voice. I could speak for the kids who were walking through the same fire as myself. Through my pain came my strength.

If I hadn't endured all the agony in my life, I wouldn't be who I am. I wouldn't be the father I am without it. I teach my children to embrace their plight, the same as Nanny taught me. Everything she ever taught me was downloaded to my spirit. She's the giant whose shoulders I stand upon.

I honor her heart's equity by stepping into my purpose as a man of faith which is another tool I've used to get over the pain of the past. Because of her investment in me, I was driven to make sure every prayer she prayed was not in vain. Her assignment was to bring me to God and let him do the rest.

Recently, just before the pandemic hit, I came to a revelation that grief is the fuel for my superpower. I believe grief can fuel yours as well. Life itself comes through the pain of labor.

When a butterfly cracks its cocoon, you can see remnants of blood before it transforms into something so beautiful. Even in the imaginary world of Marvel Comics, most, if not all, the superheroes gained their superpower through tragic events. Jesus had to be betrayed, denied, whipped, and then crucified to reach His destiny. And all three came with a guide. The butterfly had the cocoon, the superhero had a mentor, and Jesus had God. I had my nanny. God uses pain not only to protect and teach you, but to design you to fulfill his purpose.

The trials and tribulations you withstand, is the Lord battle-testing you. He has to know He can trust you in the face of trouble. In Paul's letter to the Galatians, which is in the New Testament of the King James Bible, chapter 5 verse 22 reads:

"But the fruit of the Spirit is love, joy, peace, **longsuffering**, gentleness, goodness, and faith".

Of all the fruits, longsuffering is what I experienced most. It means having or showing patience in spite of troubles, especially those caused by other people. God's love is unwavering and He'll surely reward your faithfulness and strength through times of trouble with His glory. The Word even says, "Count it all joy, my brothers, when you meet trials of various kinds." (James 1:2, ESV)

Understand the things that hurt you the most occurred for the development of your character and the fulfillment of your life. Perseverance and resilience will be the vehicles to drive you to success. Going to God in prayer is and will always be your refuge in times of trouble.

Speaking to God daily and building a relationship with Him is the best tool. But don't do all the talking, allow Him to speak back to you. He will always send his Holy Spirit to comfort you.

One of the things I do besides prayer and seeking the Word of God, I resort to my gift. I'll write. I write music or poetry about how I'm feeling. I also have an affirmation journal, where I breathe life into myself. Start a daily affirmation journal and write love letters to yourself.

Shower yourself with all the love and praise you wanted from whatever or whomever you've lost.

More often than not it subsides any pain or stress I feel and gives me motivation to move forward. Finding out what gifts God has blessed you with is imperative, for these are your earthly weapons to defeat any mental or emotional battle you face. Your gifts are usually something that bring you peace when you do it because it comes naturally and effortlessly.

Once you recognize what your gifts are, allow them to become your artillery against your triggers and traumas.

Pour out all your pain into something you love doing. Remember, your story can and will be an inspiration not only for those closest to you but for the WORLD. I thank God in advance for you and what you'll surely do for the world. Through God and your gifts, you will discover you have SuperHuman Strength.

Donnie Reed is an aspiring Author, Poet, and Orator from Boston, Ma. Donnie has a passion for being a beacon of hope for the disenfranchised and forgotten people of urban areas. He's been called to be the voice of the countless men and women who are the survivors of the War on Drugs aka the War on The Black Family. Donnie is a proud girl dad of four daughters. His fatherly and nurturing spirit led him to coaching an AAU basketball team based out of Dorchester, Ma called Team Austin. You can follow Donnie on Facebook and Instagram @DBJacob

Those who have suffered understand suffering and therefore extend their hand.

~Patti Smith

Me, Motherhood and Grief

By Te'Airra Sharma

Motherhood is the catalyst that propels you into the process of the life transformation you prayed for.

-Te'Airra Sharma

From Independence to Dependence

Lazy. Worthless. Disposable. Replaceable. Trapped. Lost. Forgotten. Unloved. Used. Useless.

These are just a few of the negative words that plagued my mind as I was forced to shift my life unexpectedly from a full-time *working* mom to a full-time *stay-at-home* mom. To outsiders, the opportunity to stay home and not work during my second pregnancy was a blessing. To me, I was trapped in a world that I never wanted to participate in. My mind couldn't comprehend how I could just be home with my children, while the mothers I loved and respected had to work and also had to take care of their children. I felt guilty that this new life was too easy. If I do not have to work as hard as my friends and the women who raised me, was I a woman worthy of being a mother? Who would I be without my job? My entire adult life and identity were wrapped up in titles: wife, mother, nurse, working mom. As an adult, I lived to work, so my self-worth was directly attached to my profession as a nurse. Making the decision to leave my job to ensure a healthy pregnancy with my daughter was the beginning of the complete unraveling of my life.

A Voice Deactivated

Around 8 years old, I believed my voice wasn't necessary to get things done. I wasn't going to talk about my feelings because no one was listening. It would be 22 years later when this belief would be uncovered during a mental health crisis and uncovering that belief was painful. In hindsight, it's clear that I had become an expert liar...a specialist in hiding my emotions about myself and others just to keep the peace. I could not see myself, and neither could most of the people I encountered daily. Expressing what was socially acceptable to the people in my environment was the way of life, so I relinquished the right to use my voice. I learned quickly that it was not safe for me to communicate my emotions. Those thoughts were reinforced as a child with common sayings from adults like "stay in a child's place", "do not speak when adults are talking", "do as I say and not as I do" and "you don't have anything to be sad about". I had low expectations to be heard about anything that wasn't "good news". And to make matters worse, I came to know that, historically, people who look like me often became targets of violence or victims of death for using their voices. I didn't want to be rejected by the people I loved, and I certainly didn't want to die, so I chose silence. Indifference began to settle in. Why should I waste my time trying to articulate my emotions to people who do not have the capacity to hear me? As time passed, it became easier and easier to stay silent. Silence became my safety. And I was okay with that.

No Escape for the Grief: Silence Tried to Kill Me

Why does this matter? I needed that same voice to speak the truth and unlock me from the prison of depression, anxiety, and suicidal thoughts I was experiencing as a mother. During the pandemic, it was the first time I came face to face with myself and my thoughts. It was the first time in my life since becoming a mother that I was still and quiet enough to notice and feel the weight of all that I had suppressed emotionally and mentally. Because I never developed the language to express difficult emotions as a child, I felt helpless, hopeless, ashamed, and isolated as an adult. There was a voice on the inside of me screaming for help, jumping up and down, sounding the alarm hoping someone would hear me. That voice was silenced by the version of me who wanted everyone around me to believe that everything was OK. I was muted and I didn't know how to get my voice back. My authentic voice was the key I needed to unlock the door that provided an exit from the emotional pain trapped inside me. My voice and my grief were trapped under layers of lies that had accumulated for the past 22 years. I didn't believe I could escape from the pain I was in.

Confronted With Truth

In November 2020, I was sitting at home in my bed at night, seven weeks postpartum holding my baby girl in my arms with tears streaming down my face, ready to die because I couldn't see a better future for my life. A life where I didn't have to live a perfect lie or pretend, I was OK when I wasn't. My two beautiful children had been my lifeline until this point, but they were no longer a source of hope for me to keep living. This was the moment I knew I was in serious trouble. I asked God to help me. I told him, "Either you have to help me, or I am going to die." I told him how miserable I felt inside and that I was tired of pretending that I was OK when I wasn't and I could no longer hide it. I apologized for trying to do things my way and agreed to live my life on His terms. At this point, I realized I had been cycling through waves of depression for the past five years and I was tired of fighting.

Since that day, I made the decision to do life God's way and I've never had another dark day like the day I cried out to him again. During my moment of confession and reconnection with God, I experienced an overwhelming sense of peace to my mind, body, soul, heart, and environment. I knew that I was going to be OK. God has loved me unconditionally, showered me with His grace and mercy, and been so patient with me throughout my healing journey. My intimate walk with God has increased my trust and faith in Him because He has never left me even though He had every reason to let me die in darkness.

Rescued From Darkness: Road to Recovery

The first instruction I received from God was to make my mental health a priority for one year and you can make the same commitment. I saw tremendous improvement in my life after making this decision to heal. The initial phase of beginning this process was challenging but doable. Perhaps, you have found yourself feeling defeated the same as I, or perhaps, you have had an experience that caused you to shrink who you are for the sake of keeping the peace. I want to share with you the process I implemented using an acronym that I hope will help you get started. That acronym is **CAR**. That's right **CAR**. Remember, we have goals to accomplish, and they require us to keep moving.

C stands for Confess. Tell God everything. He's our shock absorber for negative thoughts and emotions. God cares about what you're going through. He never wanted us to know the consequences of separation from Him, so he cares deeply about what you're going through. I recommend journaling, especially if you are new to speaking your emotions. This type of emotional dump creates space in your mind and body to receive new instructions needed for you to develop healthy habits.

A stands for Agree. You must come into agreement with God's plan for your life and for true healing. This requires you to give up your old ways of thinking, being, and doing for a new way of thinking, being and doing. It means seeking the presence of God daily, forgiving yourself and others, and making the commitment to trust God's words spoken over your life no matter what it looks like in the world around you. Agreeing with God requires you to speak. This is not something you just only think about or pray silently in your heart. You must practice speaking God's truth to and over yourself. When you speak God's truth over yourself, you start to naturally align yourself with God's will and plan for your life.

R stands for Respond. Follow the instructions He gives you and work the plan. For me, responding required a lifestyle fast to remove all distractions and influences from my life that reinforced negative cycles of emotions and behaviors. This included fasting from movies, games, social media, music, TV shows, and podcasts that were not in agreement with my healing or where I wanted my life to go. Every area of my life had to undergo an inspection. I needed to reset my mind and learn to hear God's voice. I listened to hundreds of podcasts and video teachings about mental health and God. I read books. I invested time and money to receive therapy and classes to help me with my mindset and challenge me to grow. It required me to make many sacrifices, and you may have to make some too. This is a personal decision that did not come easy.

You can do it! You can change. You can heal. You can have a new life.

The question is: Are you ready to accept and submit to the process that leads to your transformation? There will never be another version of you to walk the earth. You are unique. You are necessary. Now it's time to believe it.

There are only two choices: life or death. I encourage you to choose life.

Te'Airra loves to empower people to see the greatness that lives on the inside of them. She loves to engage in thought provoking conversations that incite positive change in the lives of the people she encounters. She is passionate about ending mental health stigma and creating mental health awareness in the lives of individuals and the community. She believes mental health crisis prevention is the key to restoring our homes and communities. Te'Airra lives in Austin, TX with her husband and two children. She loves to read, shoot basketball, and laugh. You can follow Te'Airra on Facebook, Instagram, or Clubhouse.

"For I know the plans I have for you", declares the Lord,
"plans to prosper you and not harm you, plans to give you hope and a future."

Jeremiah 29:11, NLT

Prayer of Encouragement

Heavenly Father,

Thank you to all those who were able to get a copy of this book. I pray for them as they grieve their loss, be it death, finances, job security, relationships, friendship, marriage, church hurt, or in health or spiritual death. Cover them. Cover whatever types of blocks they may experience. I lift them up to you right now and as we surrender, we know that You can take all things, even our grief and use it for Your perfect plan and Your perfect will for our lives. I pray that the people who have read this book will seek Your face and that they will bring to You their hurt, their pain, their suffering; that they will bring to You their anger, their frustration, and their questions. I pray they don't implode because they've suppressed their thoughts and feelings.

Instead, I pray that they explode with You, giving all of them to You, the safest and living Father that You are. All them a place to become transparent and vulnerable with all that troubles their hearts beyond grief.

I pray that as they go throughout their days they will continue to process through the grief and not go around, that they won't hide it and tuck it in the back of their hearts, or in their body. That they will continue to talk about it so that they can heal from it because that is the ultimate goal, and healing doesn't necessarily mean that we forget the loss, healing means that we are able to forgive it, accept the truth of what happened, and be able to use it to turn it into wisdom.

Father, I ask that You would continue to have Your way, that You will continue to meet the people right where they are as they are and that they will always come find You first in the midst of weak and weary moments. Just remind them of how much You love them and continue to be a hedge of protection around their thoughts. Continue to protect them from all hurt, harm and danger, seen and unseen; continue to cleanse their heart of revenge and vengeance because that will help them healed. Father, we ask that You continue to send the Holy Spirit to convict us, console us, encourage us, and comfort us; to give us the words to say in moments when we feel like we don't know what to do, say or ask for.

Organize our steps, so that we walk every step with and in faith moving forward and the rest of our day. Father, I pray we live with intentionality, with purpose, and knowing we were called to serve others. I ask that you continue to show us our purpose and what you want us to do; to highlight our unique abilities and talents and use those to help serve the Kingdom. Let your blessing continuously flow in and through our lives.

It's in Jesus Name we pray. Amen

Ayana Henderson has worked and consulted in the human resources field for over 10 years. As an HR professional, life coach, and communication and behavioral consultant, she has learned four things people, *specifically women*, desire most. The desire to ***find out who they truly are***, ***what they wan***t, and ***how to speak up*** and ***show up as their authentic selves unapologetically***.

Ayana has been coined, "The Generational Change Agent." Transitioning from her career in HR, her focus now is to help black & brown moms go from wounded women to warrior women.

Ayana knows that when women reclaim their voice, their value, and their purpose and when women heal they can change the trajectory of their lineage and break generational curses.

Ayana is a 5x Best-Selling Author (2x #1 Best-Selling Author) and was named a Top 20 Christian Coach and a Speaker to Watch for 2022. She resides just north of Atlanta, GA with her husband and four children. Connect with her at www.warriorwomanhood.com

Good Grief!

~Charlie Brown

Resources

BOOKS:

Permission to Feel & Heal: Courageous Testimonies of Individuals Healing After Loss By Dr. Chere M. Goode

Emotionally Empowered: The Power of Building a Better Relationship With Yourself By Charles Irving

Girl, You Are a Warrior!
A Battle Plan to Reclaim Your Voice, Your Value, and Your Purpose by Ayana M. Henderson

Grief Support Groups:

GriefShare

GriefShare is a friendly, caring group of people who will walk alongside you through one of life's most difficult experiences. You don't have to go through the grieving process alone. They offer events for a loss of a spouse and grief support, including Widowcare Find a group near you or for more information go to:

www.griefshare.org

Made in USA - Kendallville, IN
56363_9781737421221
07.31.2022 1253